Once There Were Three

Once There Were Three

Mack W. Hampton

MOODY PRESS
CHICAGO

Library of Congress Cataloging in Publication Data

Hampton, Mack W
    Once there were three.

    1. Consolation. 2. Bereavement. 3. Hampton,
Mack W. I. Title.
BV4907.H33   248'.3   77-4417
ISBN 0-8024-6063-1

Printed in the United States of America

To those who so richly blessed our family in time of direst need: our parents, Mr. and Mrs. A. J. McKenzie and Mr. and Mrs. E. M. Hampton; Dr. and Mrs. James H. Landes; and those many friends whose prayers were instrumental in the final victory which is ours today.

Contents

by Mary Lou

In the Arms of Jesus

A precious gift of God was she,
The "pet" of all the family;
No dearer child e'er born of man
Was our beloved Martha Ann.

Her lovely face and sparkling eyes
Shone with wonderment and surprise;
A cherub sweet, but impish, too,
In purest love and dearness grew.

What joy to hold her in our arms,
Delighting in her childish charms;
With busy little hands and feet
She made our happy home complete.

But she's no longer with us now,
And to God's will we humbly bow;
For He who paid sin's awful price,
Asked of us this great sacrifice.

It happened in a tender way,
While she was happily at play;
In wondrous joy we heard her cry,
"Oh, I saw Jesus passing by!

"He looked at me so lovingly,
And said, 'Dear child, come Home with Me;
I have a garden bright and fair,
With many children playing there.

'And hosts of shining angels, too,
Waiting your every wish to do.'
Oh, Mommy, Daddy, may I go?"
. . . And how her angel face did glow!

Dear one, we thought, this thing you ask
So sorely sets our hearts to task;
Yet love compelled her full release
To go where all is joy and peace.

In glorious light she walked with Him,
Our earthly vision growing dim;
With radiant smile she waved once more
Then passed beyond the Golden Door.

By faith we see her in His arms,
Protected from all mortal harms,
Playing around His sacred feet,
Hearing His voice so kind and sweet.

Though we can't fully understand,
We'll follow on, led by His hand;
And one day through God's wondrous grace,
We'll join her in that Heav'nly Place.

DELMA WHATLEY RENO

Preface

To state in words one's own victory over tragedy is most difficult in light of recurring doubts that must be dealt with over and over again. Many of our friends have expressed, "What great faith you have displayed through it all!" If they only knew how difficult it has been through these past four years to cope with an indescribable loss that cannot be eased except by God's love administered over an extended period of time!

When a family gives one of their own children back to God, the finality of it is more than heart and soul can endure—except that their faith is established in Him. As a dear friend commented, "You barely made it *with* God; just think what would have happened without Him." This writing, then, shall be an attempt to describe such a loss and discuss that which can only fill the void—faith in Almighty God.

This book is written from a layman's point of view, for I am nothing more nor less than a Christian of thirty-four years and a citizen of forty-three years. While growing up I often heard others comment, "He's such a serious-minded boy." Perhaps this is the reason I always felt strangely moved by Gospel preaching and singing. I always felt that the church, God's house, was the dearest, sweetest, most wonderful place in all the world to spend time each week in glorifying God. When we lost Martha, even after all those years of growing in grace, I was still staggered by the enormity of it all. It was then I began to understand that God must be Lord of one's life each moment of each day—now and forever.

There is untold heartache and sorrow when one parts with his own flesh and blood, even though for a season. But there is a victory which is found in Christ Jesus that is equally as indescribable as all the grief. Although all sorrow will eventually be swallowed up in the resurrection, right now there is a measure of victory for all who place their trust in Him. The purpose, then, in writing these heartfelt words is that someone, sometime, in some place of similar experience might find the strength to begin to endure until the passage of time permits God's infinite, unspeakable love and mercy to engulf like the swelling tide and make life worth living once again.

Part 1
A TEST OF FAITH

The Lord gave, and the Lord hath taken away;
blessed be the name of the Lord.
Job 1:21

To every thing there is a season,
and a time to every purpose under the heaven:
a time to be born, and a time to die.
Ecclesiastes 3:1-2

Peace I leave with you, my peace I give unto you:
not as the world giveth, give I unto you.
Let not your heart be troubled,
neither let it be afraid.
John 14:27

1

The Lord Giveth, the Lord Taketh

Martha was the third of three children, Dick and Jeff being four and three years old, respectively, when she was born at Baylor Hospital on March 2, 1962. Although Ann's pregnancy had been a surprise, the prospect of finally having a little girl was sufficient to make the early days of 1962 full of keen anticipation. Surely the seemingly insurmountable odds of having a girl instead of another boy could be broken, even though males were in the majority among family relatives.

When Martha did finally arrive, there was great joy on Salem Drive, and even Ann's doctor was elated because he now renewed his faith in his own family producing a girl baby after the first four had been boys. Ann and I rejoiced to the fullest and exclaimed with proud voices, "It's a girl!" God had given us a little girl at last—one to hold, to cherish, and to spoil.

During those early days with Martha we realized what a "perfect" family we now had, and God had done it. Once again God's grace seemed to have been bestowed upon one of His favorite young families, but we were soon to learn that God's grace is unmerited.

As I remember Martha, she was both a beautiful and precocious child. Her brunette hair was shoulder length and her skin olive. But more than this, she always had that mischievous twinkle in her dark eyes that complemented an ever present smile. She was so petite that we were afraid that her growth was behind schedule, but our doctor merely said, "She is going to be a little girl." She was small in stature but tall enough to reach the cookie jar on the highest shelf. Her look of innocence and her leadership abilities were sufficient to entrap her brothers and make them accomplices in many a caper. We loved her dearly, but we were baffled by her independence and by her stubborn desire to do everything her way.

Martha's sense of humor kept us in stitches most of the time. As the bread was passed during the Lord's Supper service at church one Sunday, she commented as the plate was passed, "Was that popcorn?" She knew better, but this was just her way. On another occasion during the observance of the sacred supper, she remarked as she sat quietly on the pew, "And the preacher said, 'One, two, three—drink your Kool-Aid.' " Many an effort to say grace before meals was disturbed by her uncontrolled giggles, for you see, everything in life had a funny side, a humorous side that demanded a response. Martha coined words to express her thoughts humorously: "kingbosage" meant large and kingly, and "spasmatack" was her word for convulsion. Therefore, a large chair, a plate overflowing with food, and a big person were "kingbosage." Anything from a loud sneeze to goofy behavior was a "spasmatack." And so Martha brought laughter into our home!

Martha never walked where there was room enough to run; this included the hall and the front porch at home. She would hit the front door with the explosiveness of a mortar shell, and she could open it with the same force. Her silent approaches were but the quiet before the storm; soon something had to give. She loved being outside and seemed to be able to transport herself in single bounds across most yards. She could climb with the best and outdistance the fastest. To grasp her little hand and escort her across a busy street took all the finesse and agility Ann and I could muster. More than once this desire to hold to and protect came back to haunt us after she had slipped through our fingers on that dreadful day to be with God forever.

To repress unpleasant thoughts and experiences is sometimes to forget much of what happened. Such has been my fate, for after Martha died I could not stand to see her picture, remember her antics, or even repeat her name aloud. Even the events leading up to her death seem so distant and vague at this time due to my persistent efforts to repress all of those hurtful thoughts and remembrances. This characteristic of man to forget and move ahead, even after death and destruction have all but ruined a life, leads me to believe that God's provision is sufficient if requested in faith through prayer. However, I shall prayerfully attempt to relate some of the details.

It was April 6, 1971, a beautiful spring day with no hint of an event that would completely change our lives and the master schedule we had prepared for the future. It was time again to drive from Richardson to Orange to visit Ann's parents during the Easter holidays. The trip would require six hours, allowing for several stops along the way. At breakfast that morning I

17

said grace and asked God to protect us all the way; I always silently prayed as we traveled on any trip of this nature. After our tragic accident I often reflected upon having asked God to "watch over us" that morning. Had God heard my prayer? What kind of a God would allow this to happen? Why pray when tragedies such as we experienced seem to be a matter of luck or chance? So many questions, but the answers would come someday.

I do remember that we were happy and lighthearted that day, and for the first time I was actually looking forward to spending a few days with my in-laws without the responsibilities of being head of the house. Also, we owned a new automobile that would make the trip that much more enjoyable. To say the day was perfect was an understatement.

I had always imagined the worst when driving along; that is, what would I do if we were meeting someone head-on or if someone were to stop abruptly in front of us, or what would I do if I lost control of the automobile? I was just not prepared for what took place as we approached Beaumont. An old Ford Ranchero driven by a seventy-year-old woman approached a stop sign ever so slowly. And then, at the last possible moment, without stopping or yielding, she continued through the stop sign and across U.S. 69 into our path. It was as though she wanted to make her automobile the best possible target for our car to hit broadside.

And we did, in spite of good brakes, good tires, and all the rest that characterize a new automobile. There was no opportunity to swerve, but if we had, we might have rolled the car and all been killed. We did what I thought was best at the time—instinctively steered straight ahead and braked hard to lessen the impact. I do not remember the impact. I remember only that two elderly people in the other automobile were killed, and our little Martha was badly hurt; she received an injury to her liver, unknown to us at the time of the accident.

Martha died from internal injuries that night at a Beaumont hospital. The dearest, most precious gift God could have given us had been taken away—so quickly and without warning. How could this be happening to us who loved God so much and had always prayed for a safe journey anytime we traveled? Why couldn't the doctor save her as he undoubtedly had saved others? Had my driving skills been deficient? Why hadn't we taken a different route when Ann was keenly aware of an impulse to turn at the fork in the road? And so began a series of "if onlys" that would haunt us for months to come.

During the immediate days that followed, a continual parade of "whys" passed by hour after hour and day after day. Could a loving God who had created her in His own spiritual image, who had cared for her for nine years of steady growth and development, who had made her a blessing to all of her teachers and friends, who had warmed my heart with the knowledge that someday I could give my daughter away in marriage—could such a God of grace and mercy now take back His own?

Although there is no pat answer to this, one of life's unanswerable questions, one does encounter God in it all, as expressed in this marvelous poem by Edgar A. Guest:

To All Parents

"I'll lend you for a little time
    a child of mine," He said,
"For you to love the while she lives
    and mourn for when she's dead.
It may be six or seven years, or
    twenty-two or three,
But will you, till I call her back,
    take care of her for Me?
She'll bring her charms to gladden you,
    and shall her stay be brief,
"You'll have her lovely memories as
    solace for your grief.

"I cannot promise she will stay,
    Since all from earth return,
But there are lessons taught down there
    I want this child to learn.
I've looked the wide world over
    in my search for teachers true,
And from the throngs that crowd life's lanes
    I have selected you.
Now will you give her all your love,
    nor think the labor vain,
Nor hate Me when I come to call and
    take her back again?"

I fancied that I heard them say:
    "Dear Lord, Thy will be done!
For all the joy Thy child shall bring,
    the risk of grief we'll run.
We'll shelter her with tenderness,
    and love her while we may,
And for the happiness we've known
    forever grateful stay;

20

But shall the angels call for her
   much sooner than we've planned,
We'll brave the bitter grief that comes,
   and try to understand."*

Although we will be taking a look at what God's
Word says about living in faith in subsequent chapters,
let me at this time humbly attempt to express my sincere feelings and beliefs as to why God took our little
Martha. First of all, there was an accident, and acci-
dents hurt and destroy. It makes no difference who we
are or what we do; if we are involved in a serious accident, then we can expect someone to be hurt or killed.
There are laws of gravity, motion, force, and a dozen
other physical laws that man cannot violate without
suffering the consequences. We were involved in just
such an experience, and if Almighty God had established a water barrier to break our speed we all would
have been saved. He miraculously saved the rest of our
family, but He took Martha. The circumstances, the
forces that were released, and the time element were
such that only God's intervention, as was true in part-
ing the Red Sea, could have saved little Martha. God
had control of the situation, but in His infinite plan for
all our lives it was time for her to go live with Him "in
His house." So my first conclusion is that it was time; it
was time for God's will to be done in this fashion in
this matter which continues to affect our lives to this
day. Ecclesiastes 3:1-2 says, "To every thing there is a

season, and a time to every purpose under the heaven: a time to be born, and a time to die."

Second, God does not look at death as we see it. The greatest reward we have to look forward to is our entry into that place Christ promised for His own. On the one hand we love the present life, but on the other hand God is preparing a place for us—an indescribable place of unspeakable beauty and peace, a place to worship God through Jesus Christ forever. If that place is what we believe it to be, would not a loving and just God want His children there with Him? Death in Christ is "with Him." If we could only see it that way.

In the final analysis, what I have just said offers little peace of mind as one contemplates the days, the months, and the years separated from loved ones. Therefore, it has to be said that all our understanding must have faith in God as its cornerstone to order and to provide, to establish His perfect way, to assist in the vicissitudes of life, and to bring that peace "which passeth all understanding" (Philippians 4:7).

In the next chapter we shall see that God intervenes in our lives more than we realize and that He does watch over us.

> "Peace I leave with you, my peace I give unto you: not as the world giveth, give I unto you. Let not your heart be troubled, neither let it be afraid" (John 14:27).

Acquaint now thyself with him,
and be at peace.
        Job 22:21

I can do all things through Christ
which strengtheneth me.
        Philippians 4:13

The Lord is my shepherd. . . .
Surely goodness and mercy shall
follow me all the days of my life.
        Psalm 23:1, 6

For I am persuaded, that neither death, nor life,
nor angels, nor principalities, nor powers,
nor things present, nor things to come,
nor height, nor depth, nor any other creature,
shall be able to separate us from the love of God,
which is in Christ Jesus our Lord.
        Romans 8:38-39

2

He Watches over Us

God did take care of our family the day of the accident, but several months passed before we realized this marvelous fact. The other members of the family hardly received a scratch, but how could this be reconciled with Martha's death? In selfish sorrow we did not rejoice in the fact that God had tenderly and mercifully spared us; we did not bother to offer thanks or praise God for His miraculous intervention. Martha was dead. God, You did not take care of us!

Words cannot express the turmoil of living with these two possibilities. It was the ageless story of the loving, compassionate God who always cared for His own and the God of indifference who "just let things happen as they might." Which God was our God, and could we prove the case for His omnipotence and omnipresence?

First of all, God did care for us in that both Ann and I were wearing our seatbelts. As I remember, I had difficulty in adjusting my belt before we left the city limits of Richardson; Ann assisted me, and, as we entered the expressway, we were securely fastened. Martha was not wearing her belt because she was constantly moving from a sitting position to one of lying down with her head in her mother's lap.

Until this day the lingering question of why she was not wearing a belt concerns me and sometimes rightly or wrongly condemns me to the point of acute mental anguish and frustration. Why did she not wear a belt during the long trip to Orange? I honestly do not know, but I have spent hour upon hour with mind and soul preoccupied with the possibilities. She moved about resisting restraint, but she was nevertheless a person to be protected to the uttermost; we felt that God would surely protect us, but we presumed upon God in believing that it just could not happen to us. Yes, God had watched over us, for Ann and I would have been seriously hurt had we not been wearing seatbelts. I now know God's hand was in this simple precautionary measure, helping us remember at a strategic time. Thank God for His divine providence!

Second, one of the most amazing things that happened that proved beyond a shadow of a doubt that God had intervened was that immediately after we had gotten out of our demolished automobile, a concerned and sympathetic couple driving a late-model automobile stopped to offer assistance. They had been trailing us for many miles and witnessed the tragedy from beginning to end. After helping us reach the hospital, we learned they were related to my wife's side of the family. They were so helpful, so kind, and so compassionate. Was their being close at hand just another coincidence, just a chance happening? Of course not! God had once again provided just the right help at precisely the proper time! And so we felt and received the comfort of good friends at a time when we appeared helplessly alone to face an experience as frightening as mind could conceive.

Last, we later found that God had watched over us through the well-trained and dedicated doctor who ministered to Martha. I am sure he did absolutely all he knew how to do to save her, but he failed to keep her alive only because he was human and suffered the limitations experienced by all men of medicine. Man has the power to set the healing processes in motion, but only God can heal. We later learned that Martha's doctor was an expert in trauma and had practiced at Parkland Hospital in Dallas. Our minds were at ease, then, for we had had one of the best doctors for our needs.

Dr. Charles L. Allen has written the following in his book, *All Things Are Possible Through Prayer:*

"Acquaint now thyself with him, and be at peace. . ." (Job 22:21). That is the only real and lasting answer to the inner tension and turmoil of man. After getting to know God and committing his life to God's will, Paul found the resources for a completely victorious life. He declared: "I can do all things through Christ which strengtheneth me" (Philippians 4:13). From the moment he realized that, he never knew the meaning of inner tension or of nervous worry about anything.

David had the same experience. There was a period in his life when he thought he didn't need God, but later he learned differently. After he became really acquainted with God, he said, "The Lord is my shepherd . . . surely goodness and mercy shall follow me all the days of my life" (Psalm 23). Coming to believe in God, automatically we lose our fear of tomorrow. When that happens we are at peace.*

27

And so we became intimately acquainted with Him that day and learned through our experience that God watches over us and that we are to have and experience that peace of mind of knowing that "goodness and mercy shall follow me all the days of my life."

Romans 8:38-39 says, "For I am persuaded, that neither death, nor life, nor angels, nor principalities, nor powers, nor things present, nor things to come, nor height, nor depth, nor any other creature, shall be able to separate us from the love of God, which is in Christ Jesus our Lord." We were not separated from God's love and care that day, although it would seem He would be inclined to turn His head in order not to view the hurt and the grief, the sorrow and tears, and the agony and death. But, God is not like that. He does view all the affliction of mankind, and He is ever present in time of deepest trouble. David said, "What is man, that thou art mindful of him?" (Psalm 8:4). God *did* see our deepest needs that day; and even though we are as specks of sand on the endless shores of the ocean, He is mindful of the desires of our hearts and the anxiety of mind and soul. His awareness is beyond our comprehension.

Some years ago I served in the United States Air Force. As I studied celestial navigation in preparing to become a navigator, I discovered that the stars of greatest magnitude had been plotted in the heavens in order that men flying through space might use the stars' known positions to assist them in determining where they were over the earth. These constellations have been identifiable to man for thousands and thousands of years; those stars appear to be just where they have always been in space, but they are constantly moving. Nevertheless, man has designed and computed exact star books to aid the navigator using the sextant to arrive at a "fix" on the earth. As if this were not amazing enough, one would only need to contemplate the infinite number of stars—some seen and some beyond the range of the strongest telescopes. There is order in the universe, and He has named all the celestial bodies. And what about man—so small and insignificant, an earthling without the splendor of the stars—could God possibly watch over him? Does He care? Does He intervene? Is our God the same as the God of the patriarchs and prophets that seemed closer than the very breath of life? Yes, He is the same; a thousand times yes! And He watches over us.

*Charles Allen, *All Things Are Possible Through Prayer* (Westwood, N.J.: Revell, 1958), p. 73.

*The righteousness of thy
testimonies is everlasting:
give me understanding,
and I shall live.*
> Psalm 119:144

*Let my cry come near before thee, O Lord:
give me understanding according to thy word.*
> Psalm 119:169

*Trust in the Lord with all thine heart;
and lean not unto thine own understanding.*
> Proverbs 3:5

*And the peace of God,
which passeth all understanding,
shall keep your hearts and minds
through Christ Jesus.*
> Philippians 4:7

3

Seeking to Understand

During the first two years following Martha's death, Ann and I sought to understand God's plan and purpose for our lives. I am sure our teenage sons found little comfort in seeing their parents so completely consumed by the event that had taken their only sister. Dick and Jeff grieved with us and for us. In their own way they understood why life around the house had been changed so markedly; they were beginning to feel that all the joy had gone out of living and that their mother and father were to always have tearstained eyes and cheeks. A smile was an exception rather than the rule, and long faces and bursts of tears commonplace. With each coming special event, such as a birthday or Christmas, we experienced the hurt of lingering memories and bashed hopes and plans. After the initial shock of our supreme loss, we were trying to understand if life could go on and must go on. Some of the letters written in those early days expressed our search for understanding.

May 12, 1971

Dear Folks:
    It has been over a month since our accident, but my longing for Martha seems to be increasing. I am still so

bewildered, frustrated, and completely shocked! I have had to learn patience over the last ten years, but this latest lesson has been extremely difficult. May the Lord help my family see life in the right perspective!

I know the day will come when we can look back with fond memories to the past—days when Martha was the bright and shining star in our family. Recently Martha had been an enigma to me; her wit, individuality, and liveliness were almost beyond my comprehension. Now, I am afraid, this is what I miss most about her. These were the characteristics which made her such a lovable personality. However, at the moment my loss and longing is like that of Christ over the one lost sheep. Again, we must patiently wait—wait for the further mending of broken hearts.

It is not necessary to eulogize Martha, but I would like to say she was the sweetest gift of God ever given to man. She was God's gift of love to us for nine wonderful years. We cried for joy when she was born because God had given us a girl—a baby girl we had hoped and prayed for. We cried bitter tears when God took her away to be with Him. She was a rare gem, a precious jewel.

Now, we had dedicated our children to God, and to God they belong. God wanted sweet Martha or He would not have taken her. As parents we are entrusted with the care of our children, but they belong to us but for a little while; they belong to God forever. With our hope in heaven and everlasting life, we have the only belief that offers comfort at this time. Martha has passed through this wilderness journey of life; I pray to God that we might have the courage to follow Him all the way.

We are a closer family now. Also, an older family—in

more ways than one. With God's leadership, the comfort of the Holy Spirit, and the love of Christ, we shall live our lives to the fullest, we shall follow Him every step of the way, and we shall be victorious, for Christ is the victory.

Now do not ever forget us in your prayers—especially now. God bless all of us, every day, until we are gathered together as His children in the perfect place where sweet Martha dwells today.

At first glance this letter appears to express sorrow and despair more than a lack of understanding. However, as I now view this writing, I can see the groping, the seeking, the feeling one's way in the dark, and the desire to have the peace of mind that comes through understanding. Still, in another letter the same search for truth continued.

September 10, 1971

Dear Folks:

To ask me to write at this time, you had better be prepared for more homespun philosophy or a rambling dissertation on the facts of life. I seem to have so much on my mind, and yet it is so difficult to express it all articulately. Some day I would like to express all my thoughts in writing and pen a short book entitled, *Martha Ann*; faith, hope, and love would be the subject matter. I trust it would be inspirational.

There are no satisfactory answers to the question, why did it happen? We ask, "Why me, Lord? Why us?" We could search the world over and never find the answers we are seeking. "Just one answer," we say, but there are none. To know is to have the mind of God. Instinctively I will go on searching anyway, and some day "face to face."

How great is the illness of sorrow, of sadness, of loneliness! It is like an albatross around one's neck. It lingers on and on. There is no place in the universe to rid oneself of this emptiness, this despair. It seems to be a terminal illness! That is, it is a part of life until death comes to blot out earthly cares.

The other day I secretly viewed my color slides of Martha; it did not prove too difficult. I did learn that I had far fewer pictures than I wished for. However, in an experience like this one sees much more with his mind's eye, and this brings the sudden flurry of tears so often present these days. I trust that memories do not fade with age, for this is all we have now. I can see her run with the animals in the yard, burst through the front door with a single bound, slip quietly through the house; and I can still hear her practice the piano, laugh in the hallway, and say, "Let's go to a nice cool restaurant." (She loved eating out.)

And finally faith. What are we to do with faith? Is it to flicker and die with that sweet child? God forbid! We will always have faith—much more than before: faith that God loves and keeps His own, that right will ultimately prevail, that we must not fail Him, that we have lives to live until we are called home, that there is a heaven for each soul to share, and praise God, a grand and glorious reunion in that day and in that blessed place.

One can readily see, after reading this letter, that you just cannot keep faith from entering the period of transition demanded by a tragic event. As difficult as times were, God in Christ Jesus was entering our lives to a greater degree, and victory would someday be ours; however, this is the message of Part 2.

Finally, the following letter—never mailed, at Ann's

request—speaks sweetly of those special days when memory is most painful:

February 23, 1972

Dear Folks:

As March 2 rapidly approaches, my thoughts once again turn to my birthday girl, all-consuming thoughts that leave me sweetly sad and lonely. Last year we took Martha Ann roller skating, along with a car full of other sweet, little girls. Dick went with the girls to offer a watchful eye and any needed assistance. While they were skating, I purchased a birthday cake and carried it home for Ann's party preparation.

Now I do not remember all the details—whether the cake was chocolate or white, whether Martha blew out all nine candles, or whether the day was sunny or cloudy; but I do remember how supremely happy we were. We did not have a care in the world—only a sweet little girl to bless us constantly. Her love, her personality, her clever ways, and her natural beauty were our joy and inspiration. I could say that only God knows how we miss her, but I believe you know too.

I know you remember the Thornton Wilder production of Our Town, where sweet Emily is allowed to return home from death on a given birthday—one single opportunity to relive a day on earth with mother and father and friends. The father, Mr. Webb, exclaims, "Where's my girl, where's my birthday girl?" And so here I am asking the same question. I am thankful the dead cannot return to earth for a single day—it would be too much. But some day, face to face, I will see her.

Now folks, my blood pressure is up, tears are on my cheeks, and I have upset myself greatly by writing this short letter. God gives us the power to repress, but letter writing offers a release that often hurts. We love you all so very much, and nothing—not even death—can change this love which is as eternal as life itself.

These heartfelt letters have been entered to express my deepest thoughts at the time of writing. They represent a conglomeration of thoughts and moods; an array of expressions of grief, despair, and a turning toward understanding. May the Lord use them for His glory!

*And who knoweth whether thou art come
to the kingdom for such a time as this?*
Esther 4:14

*And God shall wipe away all tears from their eyes;
and there shall be no more death,
neither sorrow, nor crying,
neither shall there by any more pain:
for the former things are passed away.*
Revelation 21:4

*But now he is dead, wherefore should I fast?
can I bring him back again? I shall go to him,
but he shall not return to me.*
2 Samuel 12:23

*Restore unto me the joy of thy salvation;
and uphold me with thy free spirit.*
Psalm 51:12

Be still, and know that I am God.
Psalm 46:10

4

But for the Love of Friends

If it had not been for loving, understanding, compassionate friends, we could not have lived through the early weeks of our loss. I shall always remember the Wednesday morning in April when we flew back from Orange to make ready for the funeral the following day. Several church families and the pastor met us at Love Field. They said very few words, for words would have been neither adequate nor sufficient to lessen the feeling of complete loss and hopelessness. Rather, they just put their arms around us and embraced us, letting us know in this way that they cared and wished to share our burden. Their presence and willingness to love us was enough to help us live through the second most difficult day of our lives; the most difficult would be the following day. Just as we were constantly in prayer to a loving God, telling Him of all our burdens and trials, we needed somebody "like us" to lean upon.

> I must tell Jesus all of my trials;
>   I cannot bear these burdens alone;
> In my distress He kindly will help me;
>   He ever loves and cares for His own.

I must tell Jesus all of my troubles;
    He is a kind, compassionate Friend;
If I but ask Him, He will deliver,
    Make of my troubles quickly an end.

Tempted and tried I need a great Saviour,
    One who can help my burdens to bear;
I must tell Jesus, I must tell Jesus;
    He all my cares and sorrows will share.

                                    ELISHA A. HOFFMAN

The night of the tragic accident, I had called our good friends, who were members of the First Baptist Church of Dallas. They felt led to relate our sad experience to their own pastor, who called us on that Wednesday morning and declared after only a few opening remarks, "Son, I don't see how you can stand it!" The statement at the time seemed rather unusual for such an experience; but as I pondered his words days later, I realized he had expressed his heart and soul for me and that he had related to my loss in the most sincere and honest way imaginable. His statement, then, was both a compliment to my own faith and a challenge to "keep on keeping on" in the future.

Dr. and Mrs. James H. Landes, pastor and wife of our own First Baptist Church in Richardson, spent the entire day with us. They had once again grasped another opportunity for ministering and service, for our church had suffered so many family losses, troubles, and heartaches; it was not completely unlike other churches in suburbia. Because of the marked increase in family problems during the period of his pastorate, I later came to realize that his opportunity could be likened to that of Esther in the Old Testament, "And who knoweth whether thou art come to the kingdom for such a time as this?" (Esther 4:14). And we feel he came to be our undershepherd "for such a time as this."

All the people who came by our house those first days blessed us significantly. They all contributed something of immeasurable worth. The Thompson family gave generously of their time in taking care of the details in the final funeral arrangements; without Peggy's guidance and leadership, I doubt that the plans would have been properly initiated. Later, when we just had to unburden ourselves, we knew the Thompsons would listen; their unselfishness proved to be our salvation on so many occasions. Without agreeing to eat most Sunday lunches with them, we would have had to endure the silence of our own family circle. Finally, they proved to be "doers of the word, and not hearers only" (James 1:22). For this we shall be eternally grateful.

One of the most loving and dedicated friends I learned I had a few months later was my own mother-in-law, Anna Belle McKenzie. Her insight into our suffering and into the special difficulty I was experiencing led her to write one of the most meaningful and helpful letters I have ever read, and this is the very heart of this chapter. (It has been printed exactly as it was written.)

October 12, 1971

Dear Mack:

It was good to be with you and Ann and the boys for a few days.

Of course the emptiness of the place without Martha Ann will always be there. The question Why? kept coming to my mind until a few weeks ago, when I was able to put it aside by saying to myself, "Who are you to question the doings of God?"

Mack, for fifteen plus years we have wanted you to be as a son, we have also wanted Ann to be a daughter to your parents. Since the loss of Martha Ann I've wanted more than ever to sit and talk with you, but for some reason we have not. Today with God's help I'm going to try to write some things that are in my heart, things, I think, I would say to a son.

When we got home I re-read the letters we've had from you; again I want to tell you how much we appreciate the letters, and how much we love you for writing to us.

In many of your statements you so aptly express our feelings—I'm especially thinking about your first letter, first sentence, second paragraph; you said so well the thing we all must do—"Look back with fond memories." At first we found this most difficult but now, most of the time, we can recall Miss Ann's [Martha's] cute sayings with a bit of laughter. We are very aware of what is difficult for us is many, many times more difficult for you, Ann, and the boys. But this, I think, is what God would have us do.

You and Ann, I hope, can share with the boys these happy fond memories. We must not let the rest of their lives be shrouded in the heavy grief that is in your hearts—our Miss Ann would not want it this way. She was, as you said, a "bright and shining star" in your lives (and ours). Now, since this bright and happy star

42

looks down from heaven, we (none of us) must not cast a shadow of despair and sadness between us and this precious star.

The fourth and fifth paragraphs I find filled with sweet, yet serious thoughts. "Children dedicated to God"—this is a noble thing to do—if God in His wisdom seems fit to call one of these children to Heaven to serve Him in some special way then Mack, as you said, we must know God wanted and needed our little Miss Ann, and we (Alex and I) shall pray every day, yea, many times a day for you and Ann that you will accept this as God's will and that you will, with His help go about the tasks of your chosen work in a normal way. How are we to know—this may be God's test of the depth of your (and our) Christianity.

A closer family—as a closer family you will share the joys of life as well as the sorrows that are bound to come. We are told that into every life some rain must fall—and truly the rain has fallen in your lives. The storm of grief has been so heavy and tragic (and we do share this with you) but as great as the tragedy is I think we must see a miracle or miracles.

There you were a family of five; God was ready and needed one. Had He said to you or Ann or to anyone, "Choose one for me"—no one could have chosen the one, but God took the one He needed. The other four, both parents and two boys came through almost unscathed—a miracle? I say "yes." Saved from death and injuries—for what? This, with God's help, is what we must determine.

God may not call the boys, either one or both, from this world at a young age, and their line or field of work may not be in any area of theology, but if they in this period of growing up and on through adulthood and manhood can be true witnesses of honesty, integrity, and all the other ingredients of love—if they can have these things in whatever they choose as their professions or livelihoods—they will be fine fellows and God will be pleased. I know you and Ann will help them achieve to the fullest a happy life filled with good things. Not in our lives have we ever seen finer boys and brothers as congenial.

The Bible, as we know, is full of accounts of life and death. Some life spans are long, some short. Our Martha Ann's years on this earth were short, but what joy and sunshine she brought—I firmly believe that this was the appointed day for her to leave this world and take up her abode in heaven. Regardless of where you had been I think this was the day. In my questioning "Why?" God did not speak to me—but I always came up with the feeling—Martha Ann's going at this tender age spared her, as well as her family and all who loved her, suffering and grief far greater than what you and we have.

We must all remember that nowhere in His Word has God promised us a life void of sorrow. Death brings sorrow, yet we know death is a natural phenomenon of life. Since God loved all mankind enough to give His Son (only Son) so that we might have a home in heaven, a beautiful place prepared for us by Jesus Himself—John 14—a place where all tears will be wiped away—Revelation 21:4—then it behooves us all to be ready. Let's not destroy our chance of living in this beautiful home and having the joy of being with our Miss Ann and other loved ones by looking on the sorrow of death as an illness or as a terminal illness full of hopeless despair.

There is a place and a way to get from under this loneliness and despair of sorrow. The place is right where you or we are. The *way* is to put self under and fill you and our lives full of love and service for others. (Mack, as I wrote the above I was reminded of what you said your secretary, Alice, said to you soon after the accident; it was something like this—"Mack you must get on top of this and stomp it.") That, I think, is what we all must do.

When I think of service to others, I think of the Scripture that says, "Begin at Jerusalem (home base) and go to the uttermost parts." We have all heard: the family that plays together, works together and prays together will stay together. Get involved in the affairs and activities of each other—especially the boys. In this complex world we find ourselves living in, they need all the love and patient guidance they can get. Good parents like you can give this to them.

Mack, we certainly understand your relationship with Martha Ann. Alex read this paragraph in your letter and shed tears for you. With your ability of expression I hope you will some day write a little book concerning your years with Martha Ann. Some time I would like to converse with you about this.

You both work, for this we are grateful because in your work you can take care of a lot of low moments. I also know you both are beset on every hand with pressures. Mack, I do not know too much about your work but I do know the pressures are terrific. From experience I know about Ann's pressures; to mention a few: twenty-five parents, school administrators, the work of dealing with each child fairly, and now responsible for a student's training who is to go out and teach children. May I ask that you pray for each other in your work and for those with whom and for whom you work. We as Christians believe (or should) that all things are possible through prayer. Will you try it? We always pray for you, but we would like to join you in praying for others.

We, as you, are cognizant of the fact that in grief and sorrow the world for a very short time will hear and sympathize, but the saying, "The show must go on" is a true one. Another saying as far as the world is concerned—"Smile and the world smiles with you, weep and you weep alone."

There are a few other things I want to mention: Please read I Cor. 13. I've read *The Greatest Thing in the World* by Henry Drummond; on page fifty-five he offers a challenge, and I've joined him in reading I Cor. 13 at least once a week. Wish you would do the same as a family.

Please read II Samuel 12:18-23. As you see this is the account of David's actions after the death of his child—dressed and went about his normal activities. The last sentence, verse 23, is a thought of comfort. Then read Psalm 51:12; also read Psalm 46, verse 10. I think this is the key to finding God's will for our lives.

Mack, sometime we want to see the pictures. Some of the sweetest memories we have of our Miss Ann are the ones of her activities the day we were at T.W.U. She was so happy and proud of her mom; weren't we all proud and happy? Ah! Sweet memories.

Now it seems I have about reached finis; I'm afraid this is a very disconnected letter, paper or whatever you may call it—punctuation, tense, singular and plural and other things cast to the wind. Some things addressed to you, Mack, but most to you and Ann and for the family. But whatever it is, these words come from the bottom of my heart. I hope in reading this you and Ann and the boys can feel our love for you and the depth of feeling we have for you as a family in every area of your lives.

Our love to you all,

Anna Belle

46

We shall never know on this side of heaven how many of our dearest friends constantly prayed for us during those first months without Martha. I know that I have been guilty of only praying on one or two occasions for a sick or distressed friend, knowing full well that his needs would continue for weeks to come. God expects us to pray without ceasing—for others and for ourselves. I know that we did experience that heavenly comfort that came as a result of earnest, fervent prayer that continued "seventy times seven." In other words, until God had once again intervened to bring about a temporary, if not final, victory.

In closing Part 1 of this little book, I hope to have conveyed two significant truths. First, the loss of one's child cannot be measured, evaluated, analyzed, or described to the satisfaction of many readers. However, it was important to make a simple attempt to express that which was inexpressible, to address that which was unaddressable, and to picture that which only the mind of another sufferer can see in order to leave you with a partial feeling of sadness and hopelessness. This will give the second truth the fullest impact. And this second truth is that there has to be something more, out there, far greater "than tongue or pen can tell." There has to be something beyond the horizon that can set the wheel of life moving again for those who wait and grieve. That something is a living faith—a faith that brings back to someone almost dead the firm conviction that living in Christ is sufficient for time and eternity. This is the message of Part 2.

Part 2
LIVING BY FAITH

For I know that my redeemer liveth,
and that he shall stand
at the latter day upon the earth.
        Job 19:25

But there is a spirit in man:
and the inspiration of the Almighty
giveth them understanding.
        Job 32:8

Though he slay me,
yet will I trust in him.
        Job 13:15

5

Faith in God

For every life there is both a physical and spiritual beginning; the first has nothing to do with choice, while the second depends entirely upon the exercise of this freedom given by God Himself. We cannot begin to learn of faith until we first experience God's love for us. We must be sensitive to the countless ways His love is made evident from day to day, moment by moment. Then, as the object of our faith, even Jesus Christ, the Son of God, becomes brighter and sweeter and truer, we find we have the staying power, the anchor, and the foundation which keep us in a world that tries our faith—even to the breaking point. Job was sensitive to God's matchless love and grace, and he found Him able to sustain in spite of loss and death and was able to utter one of the greatest of all declarations of faith, "For I know that my redeemer liveth" (Job 19:25). Therefore, the faith our family had in God was the beginning of our assessment of our own experience and needs, and it was the "hope" of our future.

There is more than one way to define or picture the word *faith*. But in mind and soul I see that it was a "reaching upward" to Him who reaches "downward" to touch my hand and to lift me up and sustain me throughout life. Even when I do not reach up, and when I least expect it, He will reach down and touch me; it is then that I realize and experience His unmerited grace. But to look up and to reach—therein is the experience of life that builds and anchors and welds and grows as a mustard seed. As a mortal being, God has given me an active part to play, a way of escape in a world where the corpses of those who failed without Him stand as a testimony to the foolishness of men. For all shall perish without Him, but all shall find Him able who place their trust and faith in Him.

As a family we were most sensitive to God's boundless love. Especially in nature did we encounter His handiwork, and we experienced both His creativity and love. I shall always remember the vacation Ann and I took to our Western states while Martha stayed with her grandparents. At the end of a thousand miles we had viewed a thousand marvels of nature and recorded a thousand memories of God's everlasting love. Every day brought more excitement and a profound awareness that we could not delineate the length and breadth of His goodness toward man, for it was as though we had our being in the palm of His hand; we were His, and He was ours. Praise God!

We became sensitive to God's love as we experienced our children's love toward us as parents. As little people they said and did things not unlike other children, and their love for us was but indicative of an even greater love of the Father in heaven. We saw this; we sensed the immortality of the soul and the pricelessness of life itself. There is a way with children that can bring parents to God and a faith in Him. When Martha departed from this life, we lost the sharing of our love for her and her love for us; this is what breaks the heart and dries the soul. But God's love is greater than all our losses and defeats, and by an awareness of that love we see our faith growing during the height of the most consuming storm.

Also, God's love was real in Scripture and verse, God's Word in His Book and hymns. I was always moved beyond measure by Gospel preaching and singing. To hear a God-given sermon was to be handed a gift to treasure forever. To memorize a sacred song was to hide God's truth in one's soul. To worship in God's house was to experience and partake of those things eternal. Our family had done this during all our days on the earth. Therefore, our faith had begun to grow— to flicker and then to flame as necessity demanded.

God's children cannot be denied His love. There is no abyss deep or wide enough to separate us; there is no planet so far away that man can escape His presence; and there is no sin too great to find ourselves cut off forever from that love. To be aware of and sensitive to God's infinite love is the very beginning of a faith relationship that saves and keeps forever.

Our marriage was a journey in faith and trust—in Him and one another. The coming of children into the home meant a further step in the direction of God, of touching His hand. You see, all of life is a faith relationship that knows no bounds or limits, for it is faith unto faith and life unto life. We had established a childlike faith in Him who was worthy of our trust. But the question we had was like that of the critics of Job:

would the faith resulting from so great a love endure under such pressure and storm, and would life still have meaning and purpose? Could the break be mended? Would the way of God heal the most broken of hearts and would the flame of faith burn ever so brightly? Was God's love a match for the trials of this treacherous life? Would there be victory in Jesus like nothing experienced before? Would every link in that faithful chain hold secure to the end? Yes! A thousand times yes!

Job loved God because God had first loved him. There was no turning back because of adversity and loss, for Job's faith had been established years before. His love for his Creator could not be diminished or snuffed out forever. Rather, his testing only served to strengthen that faith, and he was able to proclaim, "Though he slay me, yet will I trust in him" (Job 13:15). But Job was not left to his own understanding, for Job 32:8 says, "But there is a spirit in man: and the inspiration of the Almighty giveth them understanding." This I believe about God: in our faith we are given that which will increase our faith as long as we live and experience the love that cannot fail. Call it supernatural or whatever. But simply stated, it is God Almighty.

One day a gifted college professor stated to our class that the probability of life just happening by chance was about the same as shaking the parts of a disassembled watch in a sack and having that watch come back together again and keep perfect time. It just was not possible, and as a professor of statistics he thought he would conclude the final class session in that manner. It left an impression on my life then, but I have recounted that statement hundreds of times in the years that have passed. We did not "happen" our way into existence, for God "made" us in His own spiritual image. We are "faith" creatures, and we shall and must live in faith if we are to live at all. We should be proud to say that we have faith, for to say otherwise would mean we were letting God's life pass by.

The following chapters offer keys to life, both for those who have passed the way of our family and for those who are yet to follow. God's ways are as broad and wide as our faith, and our faith is only limited by our love for Him who died that we might have everlasting life.

So now, since we have been made right in
God's sight by faith in his promises,
we can have real peace with Him because of
what Jesus Christ our Lord has done for us.
For because of our faith, He has brought us
into this place of highest privilege
where we now stand, and we confidently and
joyfully look forward to actually becoming
all that God has had in mind for us to be.
Romans 5:1-2, *The Living Bible*

I am crucified with Christ: nevertheless I live;
yet not I, but Christ liveth in me:
and the life which I now live in the flesh
I live by the faith of the Son of God,
who loved me, and gave himself for me.
Galatians 2:20

How long wilt thou forget me, O Lord? for ever?
how long wilt thou hide thy face from me?
Psalm 13:1

6

One Day at a Time

The first two verses of a favorite hymn of mine, "Then Jesus Came," seem to set the tone for this chapter on living one day at a time:

> One sat alone beside the highway begging,
>   His eyes were blind, the light he could not see;
> He clutched his rags and shivered in the shadows,
>   Then Jesus came and bade his darkness flee.

> So men today have found the Saviour able,
>   They could not conquer passion, lust, and sin;
> Their broken hearts had left them sad and lonely,
>   Then Jesus came and dwelt, Himself, within.*

OSWALD J. SMITH

It would paint the picture of a miserable and old blind man, lost in the darkness of sightlessness, finding the answer to his lifelong desire to see, in a single, brief experience with Christ. It had only taken the touch of the Master on a single day and in a moment of time. The strength, in the form of sight, had finally come. Surely this man in the hymn had longed and

---

*"Then Jesus Came," composer, Homer Rodeheaver; author, Oswald J. Smith. Copyright © 1940 by The Rodeheaver Co. © Renewed 1968, The Rodeheaver Co., owner. All rights reserved. Used by permission.

prayed continuously for some relief, some partial vision, some hope; and fulfillment had occurred in seconds. From his experience, we learn that life must be lived one day at a time—until Jesus comes, until the burden is lifted.

During a visit to our home to boost our lagging spirits, our pastor said that some people experience a complete healing after the loss of a child, but most contend with the loss, frustration, and sorrow the rest of their lives; it required facing up to each day's problems and not looking beyond. In other words, one must live a day at a time.

The apostle Paul said in Romans 5:1-2 (TLB):

> So now, since we have been made right in God's sight by faith in his promises, we can have real peace with him because of what Jesus Christ our Lord has done for us. For because of our faith, he has brought us into this place of highest privilege where we now stand, and we confidently and joyfully look forward to actually becoming all that God has had in mind for us to be.

This verse reminds us that we have a new opportunity of a faith relationship with Christ but that becoming what we must become is an effort to be continued as long as we live; we grow in grace throughout our years on the earth, and it is done one day at a time.

If we are to experience God's grace day by day as a result of our faith and our desire to know Him better, we must experience His healing one day at a time until we can rejoice in complete or partial healing. If someone were to ask, "In a similar experience, how long would it be before some degree of normalcy returned to our family?" I would have to say, in excess of four years, for this is how long it had been since we lost Martha. However, a better answer would be: Pray as long and hard as you possibly can, read God's Word more than at anytime in your life, and above all, live one day at a time. God reveals Himself to man on a daily basis; therefore, His healing is likewise daily.

Our family had mistakenly thought that with the passing of each of those early days we could begin to see an acceleration in the healing process. Rather than that, it seemed that time was standing still and that some days were worse than others. Some two years after our tragedy, I ceased counting the days as though another week or so would make a big difference and started experiencing to the fullest all that each day had to offer. God's lesson for me and my family was to be an extended one, and to become anxious and impatient was to defeat His plan for a daily growing in grace and a continuing gift of God revealing Himself in Christ.

Galatians 2:20 says, "I am crucified with Christ: nevertheless I live; yet not I, but Christ liveth in me: and the life which I now live in the flesh I live by the faith of the Son of God, who loved me, and gave himself for me." The application again is this: We live in Christ one day at a time, and we live this life by faith. We cannot expect God to hurry up and reveal His every secret the moment we are crucified with Him in our acceptance of His Son as our Saviour.

A practical aspect of the day-by-day healing that God's grace provides is described in When You Lose a Loved One, by Dr. Charles L. Allen:

We lived at Thomson, Georgia, and at the time we were building a new Sunday-school building. One day George [who had lost his entire family in a plane crash] said, "I would like to furnish the nursery, kindergarten, and primary rooms in memory of those I love." He went on to tell how much Sunday school had meant to his little girls, and now that they were in the Father's house above he wanted to do something in the Father's house here on earth which would be an inspiration to other little girls and boys.

He bought a lot of things—small chairs and tables, a tiny organ and a little piano, toys of all kinds, a record player and a library of records, books children would like, and lovely pictures for the walls.

Now George is married again, and they have a little baby. He is working, he is happy, he is living a great life. And that is just as it should be. Sorrows and disappointments come, more to some than to others, but to some extent to everyone. But out of the sorrows come lovely and beautiful things. Those we have lost inspire us to grander and nobler living, and instead of becoming bitter, we become better. And life goes on.†

We have thus far indicated the positive side of living one day at a time. The negative side is that for most people it is humanly impossible to experience a substantial leap into the future under the circumstances of so great a loss. To do so would be to become disillusioned with the results and depressed with the prospects that God does not care or know of our plight. David in Psalm 13:1 asks, "How long wilt thou forget me, O LORD? for ever? how long wilt thou hide thy face from me?"

†Charles L. Allen, When You Lose a Loved One (Westwood, N. J.: Revell, 1959), pp. 27-28.

To walk with God is to walk daily; it is to walk humbly; and it is to walk in faith to the extent that tomorrow will bring with it an additional ray of sunshine, additional understanding of God's purpose for one's life, and new insight into God's love for His own. There are no clever or certain answers to all the whys and ifs and what-could-have-beens. Sometimes God does allow us to see a glimpse of the possible reasons for His divine providence and permissive will. But, in the final analysis, to live again after experiencing such a loss is to trust, to walk, to reach out, and to look up daily to God "who loved me, and gave himself for me" (Galatians 2:20).

If We Could See Beyond Today

If we could see beyond today as God can see,
If all the clouds should roll away, the shadows flee;
O'er present griefs we would not fret, each sorrow
    we would soon forget,
For many jobs are waiting yet for you and me.

If we could know beyond today as God doth know,
Why dearest treasures pass away, and tears must
    flow;
And why the darkness leads to light, why dreary
    days will soon grow bright,
Some day life's wrongs will be made right, faith
    tells us so.

If we could see, if we could know, we often say,
But God in love a veil doth throw across our way;
We cannot see what lies before, and so we cling
    to Him the more,

He leads us till this life is o'er, trust and obey.‡

Thanks be unto God that He has made all of life somewhat of a mystery, a journey not into "nowhere" but into "somewhere" where faith is essential and of the essence, but where God reaches down as we reach up to grasp the hand that cannot fail. Oh, that we might see that God programmed faith into our very beings and that one must live by it to live at all! We must go on trusting Him one day at a time.

‡"If We Could See Beyond Today," composer, Norman J. Clayton; author, anonymous. Copyright © 1943 in *Word of Life Melodies #1* by Norman J. Clayton. © Renewed 1971, Norman Clayton Publishing Co., owner. Used by permission.

But seek ye first the kingdom of God,
and his righteousness;
and all these things
shall be added unto you.
Matthew 6:33

Let the word of Christ dwell
in you richly in all wisdom.
Colossians 3:16a

Behold, I stand at the door, and knock:
if any man hear my voice,
and open the door,
I will come in to him, and will sup with him,
and he with me.
Revelation 3:20

For I reckon that the sufferings of this present time
are not worthy to be compared with
the glory which shall be revealed in us.
Romans 8:18

7

Perspectives of Life

After one commits himself to an effort of living one day at a time in faith, he must then decide that his perspective of life is of uttermost importance, for depression will constantly be biting at his heels, and harmful moods will debilitate the strongest of Christians. I can speak from experience, as both my wife and friends can attest; during times of deepest gloom it is altogether too easy to lose sight of God's plan for our lives. There is no more practical verse in all the Bible than Matthew 6:33 for this aspect of the healing process which calls for a determined effort to keep one's sights upon God.

It became increasingly clear as the days and weeks passed that my mind appeared completely and hopelessly confused regarding how it would all turn out; that is, whether I would lose or win, whether I could continue or give up, and whether Almighty God could take this battered life of mine and salvage it for His cause and glory. I hope the readers of this chapter fully understand that this subject of "perspective" is the easiest thing in the world to talk about but the hardest of all the disciplines to practice. How can one put God first when his heart is broken beyond repair—or so it would seem to be? How can one see that life does continue and that there is yet a purpose for our lives even though a family has lost their only daughter? It is not that we do not see the forest for the trees; rather, it is that we do not see life for the tears. Mental and soul suffering clouds the mind to the point of desiring all life to end—right then and there.

I believe God has a plan for each of our lives, but it includes Him. Can you imagine it? We cannot accept His plan for us without accepting Him, and some of us are reluctant to have Him hinder our plans for having a full and happy life. His plan always has keeping our eyes upon Him and placing Him first in our lives as its foundation; there is no other course of action, there is no other plan, and there is no other way, for He is "the way, the truth, and the life" (John 14:6).

One day I went to my doctor for a physical checkup. Much to my amazement, he said, "You appear to be depressed." I certainly was aware of my depression, but how could the doctor, on this initial visit, detect that I was depressed?

Well, depression is like eyesight; if you do not have it checked by a professional, you sometimes cannot determine your own deficiencies. I remember attending a football game several years ago before getting my first pair of glasses. I did not know that I had become nearsighted until I realized that I could not read the numerals on the jerseys; I badly needed corrective glasses. Much to my dismay, I found that I also needed to do as the hymn writer said:

Turn your eyes upon Jesus,
Look full in His wonderful face;
And the things of earth will grow strangely dim
In the light of His glory and grace.

HELEN H. LEMMEL

I had attended church all of my life, I had loved God all of my life, and I had been a Christian for nearly all of my life. But I had lost my perspective. I could not see that my closer walk with Him had to be many times closer than what I was experiencing, and that I had to step back from the abyss in order to witness the continuance of my life in the steps of the Saviour. Somewhere, sometime, in those unspeakable days I had lost the way—the tracks of God that would lead me all the way. Again, those who have traveled this way—the way of pain and sorrow—would be the first to agree on the difficulty of "keeping on keeping on."

Returning to this simple verse of Scripture, Matthew 6:33, allow me to suggest the following:

1. *Return to God's Word.* If the crisis you have suffered or if the tragedy you have experienced occurred at a time when God's Word was not a part of your daily life or reading, return, return, return! One cannot overemphasize the importance of allowing God to speak through His blessed Word. Return to God by returning to His Word.

2. *Return to God in prayer.* If you have never asked Christ to come into your life and save you for His

sake, do this first; and then commence, even as a child would learn to pray. If you have been a Christian for years but have only prayed spasmodically to Him, prayer can resolve all of life's problems; return to that quiet place and lay all at His blessed feet. You can do this right now.

3. *Major on majors.* Place the really important things first in your life—not those things that do not count for Him, that do not glorify Him, and that do not continue His glorious cause. During this time of loss, when all the world appears to be against you, let those things go that only hinder and obstruct your progress in His direction. Let your tortured mind be occupied with only those possibilities that must enhance the healing process.

4. *Return to God in His ways.* This simply means to reread the blessed Sermon on the Mount and ask God to help you be more Christlike in your daily walk with Him. One cannot read the fifth, sixth, and seventh chapters of Matthew without realizing that Christ's ways must come first in every life, that He must have the preeminence, that we must love Him more than all others, and that we must attempt to live according to the "Law" that He came to fulfill and to make a part of each life, in order that we might have that life abundantly.

When God asks us to do His will day after day after day, there is always a promise, stated or implied. In Matthew 6:33 it is, "And all these things shall be added unto you." Does this mean health? It could. Does this mean material possessions? It might. Does this mean more loving and sympathetic friends? It probably will.

Does it mean a longer life and a fuller realization of God's love? I'm sure it could. However, to me it means that God will enter every home, every building, every automobile, every place you go. It means He will be closer than any earthly father or brother and be truer than any friend. It means, somehow, in only the words the apostle Paul would use so effectively, "For to me to live is Christ" (Philippians 1:21).

In the final analysis, it means the Creator of this universe, the Maker of all men, the Saviour of this world, the King of kings, and Lord of lords will dwell in your life and heart. It means victory over sorrow, over heartache, over grief, and victory over any and all problems that man has or will ever face. In the simplest terms, it means in His way, in His wisdom, in His love, and in His victory, He will provide for your every need. Amen, and amen!

For none of us liveth to himself,
and no man dieth to himself.
For whether we live, we live unto the Lord;
and whether we die, we die unto the Lord:
whether we live therefore, or die,
we are the Lord's.
Romans 14:7-8

For to me to live is Christ,
and to die is gain.
Philippians 1:21

8

To Live or to Die

During those early months after Martha had gone, neither Ann nor I cared whether we lived or died. It made no difference, for life no longer had the same meaning as before. I remember that both of us "let things go around the house." That is, we did not bother with the "little things" that were always accomplished before the day was over. Our interests had diminished to the point that I spent as much time sleeping on Sunday afternoon as humanly possible to escape agonizing thoughts that had tortured my mind and soul for much too long. I could have cared less about how the yard looked that first summer without Martha. Why worry about these things when life had seemingly ended and time was now standing still?

Pride is often all-important to us, but when one's mind is constantly and continually occupied with thoughts of a departed child, it takes second or third place. After all, just existing is the all-important thing—the only thing. And so we found ourselves very poor examples of living life with purpose and fulfillment. Many times, amid flowing tears and bitter despair, I heard Ann exclaim, "I wish I were dead!" And bless her heart, she meant it.

Our days consisted of going to work, as difficult as that was, and coming home each evening to compare agonies. Ann's difficulty was in her role as a school-teacher of the exact age group Martha would have been in. All she could see, day after day, were little girls who, in her mind's eye, looked and acted just like Martha. They all appeared exceedingly lovable and adorable, and to have one of them show affection toward Ann was more than she could bear. Every child reminded her of Martha.

My problem was that I sought out little girls who would remind me of Martha. Why, nearly every little brunette in Dallas of the age of nine or ten reminded me of her! Also, I rode the city bus to work each day, and this gave me altogether too much time to remember and to worry and to feel that "there just had to be a way to get Martha back." As one might expect, I experienced a number of tearful dreams at night that would start the new day off on a sad note.

One dream that tore my very heart out was this: I was attending a kind of reunion where many of my friends and loved ones were. Suddenly, in my dream, the telephone rang, and some kind person on the end of the line advised me that Martha would be returning home within a few days. At first I joyously announced to the group that Martha had been visiting in another city, but that she would be returning immediately. Then, as though I had been struck by lightning, I realized that could not be so, that Martha was dead and could never come back. As the dream ended, I experienced the full force of frustration, futility, and despair. I realized that someone had made me the victim of a monstrous hoax, an unspeakable trick. I awoke with my face still wet from tears shed during the dream. I was so wrought up that I added a few more conscious tears.

Dying, then, I thought, would be the merciful way for it to all end; no more sorrow, no more tears, no more searching endlessly for Martha in the park, at school, or in the city. However, one day while listening to our city's religious radio station, I heard Philippians 1:21 quoted, and for the first time I fully understood the tremendous impact of its meaning.

Paul was saying that it did not really matter to him whether he lived or died. After all, he had in his body the scars of the Lord Jesus Christ, and he had fought a good fight while keeping the faith to the uttermost. Why should living another day matter to Paul, whom heaven may declare to have lived the greatest life on earth, second only to Christ? And when Paul pondered the everlasting reunion with God's only Son in that heaven prepared for His saints and angels—the glory and beauty of it all and a place to praise Christ forever—why would it not be better to die? Would it not be gain to lay down the persecutions, the hatred, the shipwrecks, and the loneliness in order to be forever in the presence of the Saviour? Of course it would be gain; after all, Paul had given his affirmation in the final resurrection and rewards for the saints. He knew that nothing could separate him from God's love in Christ. The apostle could say then, "Lord, I would like to be with You in paradise today—right now."

There is another side of that verse that makes Philippians 1:21 the greatest single psychological cure in the world. First, if God wants me, I am ready; but if He desires that I live, I am ready to let Christ in the power of the Holy Spirit live in me completely—every day until I die. I am ready to say that my life is His and that His life is mine. Paul is saying that life is Christ, and that Paul's life is Christ living in and through him. Oh, to live with the final and ultimate victory always in sight, to live in the knowledge that nothing can separate you from His love and care, and to live with the hope of everlasting life which begins at the very moment one surrenders his will to Him! What a joy to live the life in Christ! Paul could also say, "Lord, if You want me to keep on living, I will just keep on preaching Christ and Him crucified and point every soul I can to the Saviour of the world."

In God's time, in His will, and in His love, our family began to see that He wanted us to *live* for Him. There are still untold and unnumbered things for us to do with our lives in these times. We have learned that life does not end in the grave, and therefore life should not end for those yet living with the memories of loved ones gone. We discovered there are two parts, or two chapters, for every life—one was living and the other dying. We now know we are capable of handling either one. Furthermore, life now seems to have much more purpose than before Martha's death. We know we are ready to give our all in New Testament living; living or dying makes no difference now. The thing that matters is serving Him all the days of our lives, be they long or short.

Over a period of time, and through God's continuing revelation, life has now taken on new meaning. Because of what Christ did for me on the cross and be-

cause of the blessed assurance I have in Him, I feel as
Isaac Watts did when he wrote:

> When I survey the wondrous cross,
> On which the Prince of glory died,
> My richest gain I count but loss,
> And pour contempt on all my pride.
>
> Were the whole realm of nature mine,
> That were a present far too small;
> Love so amazing, so divine,
> Demands my soul, my life, my all.

And because He lives, I shall also live. Another amen
and amen!

It is appointed unto men once to die.
Hebrews 9:27a

Because thou hast been my help,
therefore in the shadow of thy wings will I rejoice.
Psalm 63:7

Although the fig tree shall not blossom,
neither shall fruit be in the vines;
the labour of the olive shall fail,
and the fields shall yield no meat;
the flock shall be cut off from the fold,
and there shall be no herd in the stalls:
Yet I will rejoice in the Lord,
I will joy in the God of my salvation.
Habakkuk 3:17-18

Rejoice in the Lord alway:
and again I say, Rejoice.
Philippians 4:4

9

When Death Comes

The final enemy, death, always brings heartache, sorrow, and separation. We cannot escape the final chapters to our lives; neither can we elude the sharing of suffering by others. With each tick of the clock someone somewhere is crying his or her heart out, for he has witnessed and experienced the close, the finale of another life, and he was helpless to intervene, and frustration and loss once again proved greater than will or emotions. Death is no respecter of persons, and a just man, a righteous man, a known man, or a rich man is just as dead at the time of death as an evil man, a godless man, or a wasted man. And the final enemy *is* death, for "it is appointed unto men once to die" (Hebrews 9:27).

In spite of the gloom shed upon the horizon at intervals throughout our lives and in spite of the despair that floods our souls at one moment or another, God holds the keys to our equilibrium in His hand, and they are ours if we reach out in belief and in faith. The first key is that in death there is also life, and the other is "that in all things we should rejoice."

I shall always remember the elderly, saintly landlady who, in June 1952, rented two rooms to college boys. I was fortunate to have found her place that hot summer before my freshman year. She could not believe I was moving into the front room of her modest little home, where west windows made the heat much more unbearable. Noting immediately that I had only an electric fan with me, she brought to the door the largest pitcher of ice water she could find. I can still see her as she stood there, wondering, I am sure, if I would survive the summer. Thus began our relationship, and she showed a compassion and a concern that live in my memory to this day.

One day she became ill and died quite suddenly. Her husband and married son had died tragically some years before, and she was lonely at the time of death with only a daughter-in-law and granddaughter to comfort her during those last hours in the hospital. I visited her that final evening. As I left to return to my little room on South 6th Street, it dawned on me that there is both life and death in any hospital. Babies are being born in one wing, and life ends in another part. The one is just as much a part of our experience as the other; and in God's infinite plan, life seems to spring forth from death. We plant seeds that for all practical purposes are dead, unless they find their way into soil. Then there is a sprouting, a growing, a blooming. We see examples of this in both plant and animal life; one life ends but another begins.

And so that night I understood that God had balanced the scale of our existence just as He had balanced all bodies in the heavens and in the earth. For you see, at the death of a loved one there should come a rebirth of spirit, a rekindling of hope, and a new determination to live a better life in Christ. Death can mean a fuller, a nobler, and a more fruitful life in the future. The birth of many a glorious hymn or poem has come as a result of death—of a son, a daughter, a wife and mother, or a husband and father. Many times death is the beginning—certainly not the end—to a seemingly tragic story. New interests are aroused, new goals and challenges are accepted, new forces are released, and for the first time man may find himself—and his Creator.

If someone special dies and we are not able eventually to see that God does have a plan for our lives and that "something" somehow reflects our experience with that "someone," we are poor indeed and without hope in this life. We must reach up and claim this key, this truth, if we are to survive. And God will surely point us to His Son whose death brought life now and forever to all who believe.

The second key, that in all things we should rejoice, is nothing more or less than the greatest advice possible for the period immediately following the death of a loved one. The apostle Paul had experienced enough of life to know that one does not survive in this world with slumped shoulders, a sad expression, and a defeated and depressed spirit. Rather, it is best to accept those things we cannot change and to thank God for that which we do have, for everything comes from God. Many times "praise" is the only weapon we have to defeat despair, and without it we would perish. Counting our blessings at the time of defeat and loss is a most unusual thing to do, but it is the only thing we must do.

At the funeral service for a dear and godly aunt, the

pastor used as his text, "That in all things we should be happy." This was perhaps the most remarkable sermon that I had ever heard for such an occasion, and it gave me a lilt and a lift that were inexpressible. My mind was immediately captured when he read the text, for I wondered how that verse could be applicable in such an experience. However, as he continued to develop the theme and its meaning, I, too, began to rejoice and be happy as I remembered her life and her faithfulness to my uncle for forty-one years. There was reason to be glad in the memories and accomplishments of the past, and there was no better time to recount them than at that memorial service. What a glorious prescription for the aches and pains produced by a broken heart, for our hurts begin to mend when we rejoice.

If someone had placed a "praise" book in our hands during that first year without Martha—a little book to encourage the counting of blessings, and the living instead of the dying in the matter—I am sure we would have set it aside for the second or third year of our experience; it would not have had the impact and perhaps would have been misunderstood. However, with the passage of time the two keys became ours, and we knew then that when death comes there is a way of escape; it is in an awareness of Him who "loved us and gave himself up for us" (Ephesians 5:2, NIV).

It is difficult to rejoice with a broken heart, to be happy without a partner or child. But it is there in God's Word and, praise God, it is true! Experiment with this truth, reach up for it, try it, claim it, and use it. It may not seem to work when early used, but keep on trying, and finally you, too, will be counting your blessings instead of your tears. You will begin again to think about life instead of death, and you can be "you" again, with hopes and aspirations, with dreams and ambitions. God has a plan for our lives, including all our griefs and tragedies, and we have but to reach up and believe.

Rejoice, for there is new life and a new beginning!

He is not here: for he is risen, as he said.
Come, see the place where the Lord lay.
Matthew 28:6

Even so, come, Lord Jesus.
Revelation 22:20

10

He Is Risen

As we come to the last chapter, I trust that you have already sensed the diminishing of sorrow and gloom and the increasing of victory which is ours. It is for all of those who believe on His name. In Christ there is no defeat, only victory, over all the trials of life; yes, even victory over the final enemy, death. There is a contemporary Gospel song that says:

> Because He lives I can face tomorrow;
> Because He lives all fear is gone;
> Because I know He holds the future,
> And life is worth the living just
> Because He lives.*

WILLIAM AND GLORIA GAITHER

The theme, then, of this chapter is: I can face tomorrow because "He is risen."

Martha is buried in the "Garden of the Cross" in a large Dallas cemetery. Selection of the site was made so quickly out of necessity that we did not realize how

---

very acceptable the place was. There is a large cross which is the central monument of that garden, and it is located on a gentle rise in the terrain. One does not realize how beautiful a site is until a loved one is placed there. However, the thing that buoyed our spirits was the sight of another monument some forty feet away, a replica of the empty tomb with the angel and inscription, "He is not here; He is risen." Each time I visit the little grave and turn to leave, due to the location my eyes always fall upon that open and empty sepulcher and that blessed inscription. Therefore, I know that my visit to that cemetery is but symbolic of my love for her and nothing more; for her spirit is risen to be with Christ. She is not there; she is risen.

This truth of my faith, and I trust of your faith, should be enough in itself to encourage the down-hearted. Without Christ, the hope of glory, life and death would be sad affairs to leave us depressed and miserable beyond description. I could not face tomorrow; I could not stand to be around people who shared this hopelessness. Life would be intolerable; it would not be worth living. But He lives!

Facing tomorrow is not the easiest task or challenge confronting us; in fact, for many it is nearly impossible. Let me state again what I said earlier: I almost failed, even with Him. I cannot conceive of men and women starting life together, and later having children, and not having Christ in the partnership. There are a multitude of little problems to resolve, and Christ should be asked to help in those decisions. But there are momentous and traumatic concerns that require the wisdom of God, and if you do not know Him you cannot possibly know His wisdom. My appeal, then, is to accept Christ now for the sake of your soul, for the sake of your family, and for the eternal influence you can have. Trust Christ to sustain you in every difficulty and to rejoice with you in every victory. He is ready, He is willing, and "whosoever will, let him take the water of life freely" (Rev 22:17). His gift of salvation is free, and He is "not willing that any should perish" (2 Peter 3:9).

What a glorious opportunity we have to live for Christ! Since I can now face tomorrow triumphantly, there is no hindering my setting out to serve. With Christ as the Lord of my life, there is no longer reason to delay being a doer of the Word. Our lives must now be devoted to giving rather than receiving, serving rather than being served, ministering rather than being ministered to, and loving with that *agape* love of God rather than receiving the love that requires something in return.

There is one last thing to be said: I can face tomorrow because He is risen, but He also shall return. If His resurrection were not enough, one could still say triumphantly and with excitement, "He shall return." When I think of the glorious possibility that He could return for His Church at any time, I can hardly stand it! The disciple that Jesus loved, John, said in the next to last verse in the book of Revelation, "Even so, come, Lord Jesus" (22:20). This should be the cry of Christians around the world and that which motivates them to point others to Christ.

Christ Returneth

It may be at morn, when the day is awaking,

When sunlight through darkness and shadow is breaking,
That Jesus will come in the fullness of glory,
To receive from the world "His own."

O Lord Jesus, how long, how long
Ere we shout the glad song,
Christ returneth! Hallelujah! hallelujah!
Amen, Hallelujah! Amen.

H. L. TURNER

I have honestly, prayerfully, and joyfully given my testimony to the fact that He has brought victory to my life and family. It has been difficult beyond words to reach the crest of the hill, for the uphill climb involved struggle and challenge for the strongest of hearts, but the downhill descent meant peace at last. Be not deceived by all that has been written. Final victory must be earned by the faithful; it will not fall like a star from heaven. A passive role will not suffice. Where a broken heart is expected, a broken spirit leads only to uselessness and futility. God can heal the wounded heart, but man must "hold tight" in attitude and spirit. This requires the efforts of all—family, friends, and church.

God has planned victories for us all. He would not have any of us fail in this life or the next. Life must go on for every fellow traveler, even as the Spirit of Christ lives in our hearts and souls. We are all in the business of living today—now. Furthermore, we have no assurance that a second or third tragedy will not befall us— only faith that God is able to provide the needed strength. To live again is to be better prepared for the unexpected to come. Certainly there is truth in the statement that "life is worst at best but eminently worth living." And live it we must.

86

Will you accept Him today and trust Him with your life, your family, your all? To know Him is to experience life in a victorious manner, and to accept Him now will begin an adventure in faith that surely and ultimately will end at the feet of our blessed Lord—in heaven, forever and ever. May the Lord bless your decision, right now!